Tip!

Written by Caroline Green

Collins

map

pin
. . .

map

pin

man

sit

...

man

sit

dip

tip

dip

tip

 Review: After reading

Use your assessment from hearing the children read to choose any GPCs and words that need additional practice.

Read 1: Decoding

- Turn to page 10 and ask the children to read the word **dip**. Ask: What is dipping?
- Turn to the "I spy sounds" pages (14–15) and ask the children what they can see in the picture that starts with the /t/ sound. (*trees, tree trunks, toad, tortoise, tiger, table, table cloth, tangerines, tea pot, tea cup, tea, toast, table, teddy bear*)
- Ask: Can you see anything in the picture that has the /t/ sound in the middle or end of the word? (*helicopter, roots, toast, pot*)

Read 2: Vocabulary

- Go back over the book and discuss the pictures. Encourage children to talk about details that stand out for them. Use a dialogic talk model to expand on their ideas and recast them in full sentences as naturally as possible.
- Work together to expand vocabulary by naming objects in the pictures that children do not know.
- Ask:
  o Where does the helicopter dip the bucket? (*water/river/lake*)
  o Where does the helicopter tip the bucket? (*on the fire*)

Read 3: Comprehension

- Discuss the picture on pages 14 and 15. Point to the helicopter and ask: What is this doing?
- Ask: What else can you see in the picture? Encourage the children to describe the objects.
- Ask the children why they think the helicopters are needed to help put out the fires. Ask: Have you ever seen a helicopter? Where was it? What was it doing?